Woman in Progress

The Reflective Journal for

Women and Girls

Subjected to Abuse and Trauma

Created by

Dr Jessica Taylor (FRSA)

Copyright © 2020 by VictimFocus (Dr Jessica Taylor)

All rights reserved. This book or any portion thereof may not be reproduced or used in any manner whatsoever without the express written permission of the publisher except for the use of brief quotations in a book review or scholarly journal with appropriate citation.

Book cover design by Johnson Marketing.

First Printing: January 2020

ISBN 978-0-244-53909-2

Dr Jessica Taylor T/A VictimFocus

Derby, UK

www.victimfocus.org.uk

Email: Jessica@victimfocus.org.uk

Ordering Information:

Special discounts are available on quantity purchases by corporations, associations, educators, and others. For details, contact the publisher at the above listed address.

This journal is dedicated to the millions of women and girls around the world who are routinely subjected to abuse, violence, torture, harassment, rape, forced marriage, mutilation and exploitation.

The millions of women who are living their lives as best they can whilst trying to process the violence and misogyny committed against them, often without support or compassion.

You have my total respect, love and support.

Special thanks to Jaimi for her support and ideas whilst developing this journal. Thanks to all the feminist activists who work every single day to support women and girls subjected to violence, abuse and trauma.

Contents

How to use this reflective journal	5
Writing about abuse and trauma	9
Memories of abuse and trauma	26
Grooming processes and experiences	48
Impact of the abuse and trauma	72
Trauma responses	99
Coping mechanisms for abuse and trauma	120
Victim blaming and self-blame	138
Blame the abuser	169
Sex and intimacy	179
Pathologisation and medicalisation of women and girls	200
Sexism, stereotypes and misogyny	214
My advice to women and girls	231
A letter to…	245
Who I am today	264
Draw yourself	281
Where to seek support	299

How to use this reflective journal

A foreword by Dr Jessica Taylor (PhD, FRSA)

Welcome to your new 'Woman in Progress' journal.

I designed this journal for every woman and girl who has been subjected to sexual or domestic violence at any point in her life. Research suggests that around 1 in 3 of us will be raped or attempted to be raped in our lifetime. Similar statistics are found in domestic violence research, in which it is reported that 1 in 3 of us will be abused by someone we love.

Further to this, we know that around 1 in 4 girls will be sexually abused in childhood.

I think it remains important to state that for most of us, the abusers are male. Every year, men make up between 97-99% of all people convicted and charged with sexual offences.

These statistics make for pretty depressing reading, but there is another way of looking at them.

The alternative is to look around you and see that you are surrounded by women and girls who have been through abuse and violence, too. So many of us are working through our traumas, exploring our feelings, rebuilding ourselves and pushing through each day after being violated, oppressed, bullied, abused, and manipulated. We are doing all of that whilst holding down jobs, attending education, bringing up children, pursuing our dreams, volunteering our time and learning how to take care of ourselves.

Women in progress are awesome.

Everyone processes sexual and domestic violence differently. What takes one woman 6 months to think through might take another 15 years. Some women will process it all at once and others will be triggered repeatedly over many years; each time processing something new that they had blocked out or misunderstood. This is completely normal and will be explored in this journal.

Responses to trauma are all unique, too. Every woman will have a different response to the violence she was subjected to. Every woman will seek to cope with those traumas in different ways. Whilst one woman might drink to cope with the memories, another woman might throw herself into weightlifting competitions. Coping mechanisms are important to explore, especially as we seem to celebrate some strategies (working hard, being a perfectionist, becoming a high achiever) and discourage others (self-harm, self-isolation, drinking alcohol). But what we rarely talk about is that whether the coping mechanism is perceived as socially acceptable or not, it still means the woman is trying to cope with something that hurts her deeply. The woman who threw herself into her career to cope with the domestic abuse is as traumatised as the woman who cuts her skin to cope with the memories of the rape. Both women need support and understanding. There is no 'right' way of coping with trauma from interpersonal violence.

What we do know for certain, is that many women and girls never disclose the things that were done to them – meaning many women cope alone. Some women cope alone for most, if not all their lives. Recent statistics suggest that only about 13% of us ever report abuse to the police, and the conviction rates for rape and sexual assaults are at the lowest they have been for decades.

It is also common for women and girls to struggle to find support or feel anxious about telling a professional what was done to them. We cannot underestimate the power it takes to lift the phone, send the email or turn up at the women's centre to seek support. Many of us never do it.

Over the 10 years I have worked with women and girls subjected to sexual and domestic violence, I have met thousands of women and girls who needed strengths-based, feminist, trauma-informed support to process the violence committed against them – but it is hard to access in some places and non-existent in others. In some places, strengths-based, feminist, trauma-informed practice is decades away and instead; women are pathologised, medicated and criminalised for being traumatised by sexual and domestic violence.

With all this in mind, I decided to create the 'Woman in Progress' journal.

We are all a work in progress. We are all a woman in progress.

Working through the memories, feelings, impacts, injuries and experiences takes time. I created this journal so that you can reflect on the abuse you were subjected to, in your own time, at your own pace, in your own space. Whether you are currently accessing therapy or not, whether you would like it one day, have had years of it or would avoid it at all costs – this journal is your personal space to explore your own experiences and start to work through them on your own terms.

Inside this journal are 16 sections of reflection questions that are designed to help you explore your own experiences, thoughts, feelings, dreams, fears, coping mechanisms and trauma responses.

You can use this journal however you like. There are 300 pages of reflective tasks which include sentence completion, doodling, lists, questions and anecdotes. They are split into sections and each section begins with an explanation of the types of tasks that are included.

It could be that you flick through the journal until you find a task that really jumps out at you or resonates with how you are feeling that day.

Alternatively, you might decide to work methodically through this journal and complete one task per week. You could also read the contents page and then choose which section you want to complete. You may even want to use this journal alongside therapy and take it to sessions to discuss your answers. The choice is yours.

You can shout, swear, challenge yourself, challenge the system, cry, celebrate and big yourself up in this journal. You can rage at the abusers. You can question the justice system. You can invest in yourself and your self-care.

You can read a question and come back to it another day. You can choose to answer 5 questions in a day if you need to work on something that is bothering you.

This journal contains difficult, challenging, critical and interesting questions. It is designed for those who feel ready to explore feelings and thoughts about abuse that can be uncomfortable and distressing. It is a courageous step to take. To decide to delve into the memories, feelings and experiences of trauma takes courage, patience and self-love.

You may need to take regular breaks from this journal and consider how you will take care of yourself whilst investing in your journey. I do not believe that women require supervision or professional support whilst they use this journal, as this just further infantilises and controls us. However, it is wise to acknowledge that some of us may well need someone to talk to whilst using this journal.

From one Woman in Progress to another, I hope that this journal helps you to process the abuse you were subjected to at the hands of others. You were never to blame, and you never deserved it. All the blame and shame sit squarely with the abusers.

You are much stronger than you realise.

In love and solidarity,

Writing about abuse and trauma

The first section of this book has been designed to help you write about the abuse and trauma in your own words, before starting any of the questions in specific sections.

If this is the first time you have ever written about the abuse and trauma you have been subjected to, it can be a mixed experience. It is normal for writing to feel cathartic and useful, but it is also normal for writing to feel stressful, triggering or exhausting. You may need to pace yourself whilst engaging with this journal and take good care of your wellbeing whilst writing.

Remember that this journal is by you, for you. It is not for anyone else. Your answers, experiences, descriptions, words, phrases and feelings are yours. This journal is not written for the eyes or minds of anyone else. It is a private space to process trauma in your own way.

For lots of women and girls, this will be the first space they have ever had to catalogue the abuse they were subjected to, when it happened, how it happened and how it made them feel. This might be the same for you.

Sometimes, seeing it all written down in ink can be unnerving. It might suddenly look like a lot more than you realised had happened. It might even feel impossible to write about years of systematic abuse, or multiple abusers.

Similarly, drawing timelines and trying to order the abuse or traumas can be difficult tasks. You might wish to map it all out on scrap paper first. Many women and girls who attempt a timeline will go through many versions before settling on one. This is usually because as they try to order the events, they remember more events – or they realise they were younger or older than they thought they were at the time of the abuse. This is completely normal. Give yourself time.

It is important to listen to yourself as you write. If you need to swear, use an offensive word, talk about something private or rage at someone – that is your choice to do so. This is your journal, and no one ever has to read it or know you have it.

Finally, as with every section and question in this journal, you are not required to complete them or answer them. You might decide that you never want to write down exactly what was done to you – and that's fine. You might never want to see a timeline of the trauma and abuse and so you can skip any questions or sections that feel uncomfortable or intimidating.

More recently, we are being encouraged to talk about abuse and our mental health or trauma, but naming the abuser is still considered a dangerous and taboo thing to do. It may be the first time you have written about the abusers in detail – indeed, I chose to include a section about blaming the abusers for everything they ever did to you and others. It might feel strange writing about them so openly for the first time, but of course, if it is safer to use initials or nicknames, do that instead.

1. How are you feeling about writing in this journal?

2. What are you going to do to look after yourself whilst you work through this journal?

3. How and when are you going to use your journal?

4. What do you want to gain from using the journal?

5. In your own words, what happened to you and who subjected you to that abuse or trauma?

6. When did it start happening and how long did it happen for?

7. Write about a time when you were sexually harassed

8. If it helps, write a list of everything you remember the abuser doing to you or saying to you

9. Draw a timeline of the abuse or traumas

10. Write about a time when you were forced to do something you didn't want to do

11. Who let you down and how did they fail you?

12. What do you remember most vividly about the abuse?

13. What did you think was happening when you were being abused?

14. Who hurt you and what did they do?

15. How has it felt to write about the abuse and trauma? Do you need to do anything differently as you work through the rest of this journal?

Memories of abuse and trauma

This section contains questions and thinking tasks about the memories you have of abuse, trauma and assaults. It aims to help you recognise which memories trigger particular feelings, thoughts or responses.

Women subjected to sexual violence are often given messages that they should stop thinking about the sexual trauma after a set amount of time. Maybe people have told us that a year is enough, ten years is enough, or thirty years is enough. The reality is, everyone is individual, and it is likely that we will keep processing our trauma memories throughout our lives.

We will think about them sometimes, and other times we will not. We may spend some time reprocessing trauma memories if we have been recently triggered by something or someone.

There is no set time limit on trauma or our memories. There is no shame or guilt in thinking about or needing to talk about what happened no matter when it happened or how long ago it was.

Women and girls who ring rape and sexual violence helplines are typically anywhere between 10 years old and 90 years old. Many volunteers and staff members working on those helplines have talked to women decades after the abuse took place. This is completely normal.

Memories of abuse, rape and trauma can sometimes come back to us many years later.

Life events of all different kinds can trigger us to think about trauma memories. This is normal and rational. Before I talk about why this might happen, I have supplied a list of life events that commonly trigger us to reprocess or think about sexual traumas and abuse we were subjected to:

- When we have sexual experiences with others
- When we start new relationships
- When we become pregnant or have children
- When we need medical treatment, operations or medical examinations
- When our children begin to get to the ages we were at when we were abused
- When we meet people who trigger us or remind us of the abuser(s)
- When we go to family gatherings and occasions where the abuser or their family will also attend
- When we must trust others to take care of us or our children
- When the abuser becomes ill or dies
- When our parents or carers become ill or die
- If we find out that the abuser had other victims
- If the abuser goes on to have children or grandchildren themselves
- If the abuser is arrested or tried for other crimes

This is not an exhaustive list, but it is common for events such as these to trigger us to think about sexual trauma. It may be that the feelings of the life event make us feel the same way we felt during the abuse. However, it could also be that the life event forces us to think about the sexual trauma differently.

For example, it is common and normal to reprocess childhood trauma when you have your own children. It is also normal to become upset around the time your children reach the ages you were when you were abused.

Use this section to write about the memories you have of the abuse and how you feel about those memories.

Remember to take care of yourself and not to do too much at a time.

1. Write about the memories that keep coming back to you

2. Some memories feel like they replay over and over in your head. Do you have any like that?

3. Which memory have you tried to block out and why?

4. Write about a memory that makes you feel angry. Who are you angry with?

5. Which memory makes you feel scared?

6. Write about the blurry memory you have. Are you glad it is blurry, or do you wish it was clearer?

7. Some memories can be confusing. Do you have any memories of abuse or trauma that confuse you or seem to make little sense?

8. When you remember the abuse, where are you in the memory? Are you looking down at yourself as if you are an onlooker, or are the memories in first person?

9. Which memory causes you to feel guilt or shame?

10. Write about a positive memory at the time of the abuse. How does that memory make you feel now?

11. Which memory hurts but you would never want to erase?

12. One memory I struggle with is…

13. If you could erase all the memories of the abuse and trauma, would you do it?

14. Did any of your memories of abuse come back to you suddenly later in life?

15. Write about a memory that was triggered by something

16. I wish I could remember more about…

17. What is your earliest memory of abuse, harassment or assault?

18. Do you try to block out memories or do you engage with them? Why?

19. How does it feel when people question your memories of abuse and trauma?

Grooming processes and experiences

This section contains questions and tasks that ask you to think about the tactics the abuser used to groom, manipulate and control you.

Generally, when people talk about grooming, they usually mean the process that an abuser uses to manipulate and control their victim. Grooming is a very diverse process, however. It does not follow stages and there is no 'blueprint' for how abusers groom someone.

For example, some women may have been groomed using romantic tactics like gift-giving, compliments, spending time together, being told they are special, being told they love them, encouraging them to keep secrets and being promised relationships in the future. However, some women may have been groomed using violence coercion, threats, lies, manipulation, gaslighting, mind games and turning everyone against her until all that is left is the abuser. Grooming is often a combination of these tactics and can shift and change throughout the abuse.

Sometimes abusers will begin with romantic gestures and mimic a relationship before moving to threats, violence and mind games. Other abusers may prefer completely different tactics, such as exploitation or extortion. They might notice that a person is homeless and struggling for money and offer them somewhere to stay but only if they give them sex.

Grooming can take days, weeks, months or years. Every abuser will have a different way of grooming and manipulating women and girls. Most can switch their tactics and control methods, too.

Grooming is not a specific behaviour or skill that only offenders and abusers have. This has been one of the biggest myths that has affected our understanding of grooming. Because we have often seen grooming as specific to sex offenders, we have not noticed that grooming occurs in lots of different contexts and is used by lots of different people.

Grooming is a social behaviour used by everyone. Everyone grooms everyone else. We groom children, we groom our friends and prospective partners. We groom our employees and colleagues. In turn, we are groomed too. We are even groomed by society, fashion, marketing, the government, authorities and media. This is because grooming is simply a behaviour that seeks to influence and manipulate others into doing something, thinking something or feeling something. Sometimes it can be used positively and sometimes it can be used negatively.

For example, consider the grooming process of teaching children how to behave and succeed in school. When we first get to school, we have never experienced such a large group of children our own age, all crammed into one room with one adult in charge. We may have never been away from our parents before. We will have never worn a uniform to match everyone else before. When we arrive, we know nothing of the social etiquette of school. We do not know that we must sit cross legged on the floor. We do not know that we are supposed to be quiet. We do not know that we should line up in pairs to get into the classroom. We do not know that we are supposed to sing in unison in assembly. We do not know that we are supposed to put our hand up before we speak to an adult.

These behaviours are alien to us, and we do not understand them. However, we are groomed to behave and think this way as soon as we enter the school.

We are punished if we do not do the things that are asked of us and we are rewarded when we do the things that are asked of us. We might be split up from our friends if we do not do what the adult is asking. We might be told off or made to stand by a wall. We might be ignored or told to be quiet if we speak out of turn. Over a period of time, we are groomed using both punishment and positive reinforcement, until we behave exactly the way they want us to.

When we think about grooming like this, we begin to realise that we have been groomed to perform behaviours most of our lives. In fact, much of the world's systems and institutions rely on grooming. Indeed, all marketing and advertisement relies on grooming us to believe that we need or want the items or services they are selling.

Why didn't I spot the signs of grooming when it was happening to me?

When you look at grooming as the huge, global use of social tactics like in the section above, it should become clearer as to why we don't notice when we are being groomed for abuse. If many of us have been groomed our whole lives by our parents, teachers, colleagues, friends and family - then why would we spot the signs of grooming when someone was doing it to harm us?

Most grooming processes feel the same up until we figure out that the person has bad intentions. It is common for us not to know we are being groomed. Children and adults find it hard to identify a grooming process. We may have been through them many times, but they feel so familiar that we do not easily figure out what is happening to us.

For example, have you ever had a friend who you thought was brilliant and considered them a really close friend until they suddenly started to belittle you, argue with you, lie to you and bully you? Maybe they started to wear you down over time or make you feel bad about yourself? Or maybe when you needed them most they were nowhere to be seen when you had supported them through stuff in their own lives?

Often with people like this, we ask ourselves, 'How did I not see it coming?' or 'How did I let them manipulate me like this?'

This is the same as being groomed. We can be misled, manipulated and harmed by people without our knowledge. This is even more pronounced in relationships where we really love or care about the abuser - as we may find it even harder to spot the signs of grooming.

The grooming process felt good and I enjoyed some of it, what does that mean?

In short, it just means that the abuser was very skilled at making you feel as if you enjoy the things they were doing. Some abusers are capable of this, and might deliberately give you compliments, gifts, spend time with you, treat you nicely and flatter you in order to get what they want. You might have been to nice places, done exciting things and enjoyed events or time together. This is common and is nothing to be ashamed about. The most important thing to remember is that they were deliberately creating these experiences as part of the grooming process - so there is no shame or blame for you. They hold 100% of the blame for this.

I knew I was being groomed but I couldn't escape or find a way to stop it. Is this my fault?

This is not your fault. Lots of women get to the point where they start to see that they are being groomed, lied to and manipulated. Some even start to realise they are being raped and abused. However, that realisation doesn't always mean that they can leave safely or quickly. For children being abused by parents and carers, there is often no safe way out. For adult women being abused by partners or spouses, there are often practical issues that keep them trapped in abuse such as finances, property, children, family pressures, debt, illness or dependency.

Sometimes, when women try to escape an abuser, the abuser escalates their behaviours and the abuse or rapes will get worse. For this reason, lots of women feel that they cannot leave or escape because they fear what will happen next. These are real, rational fears.

Being trapped with an abuser is never your fault. They are 100% to blame for making you feel trapped. In some cases, abusers will deliberately make you feel this way and the main aim of their grooming is to keep you from leaving.

1. How did the abuser make you feel?

2. If you were abused by multiple people, how did their grooming strategies differ?

3. What did the abuser do to make you feel good or special?

4. List all the tactics the abuser used to manipulate and control you

5. What untrue things did the abuser make you believe?

6. How did the abuser make you feel wanted?

7. How did the abuser threaten you? (Threats can be physical, emotional, social or psychological, direct or indirect)

8. What did the abuser do to keep you from telling someone what they were doing?

9. How did the abuser use positive or 'nice' tactics to groom you?

10. List all the ways that the abuser made you feel

11. How did the abuser to make you believe you were powerless?

12. How did the abuser make you think you wanted it to happen?

13. How long did it take for the abuser to groom you to be compliant?

14. How did the abuser earn your trust?

15. When did you realise you had been groomed and how did that realisation happen?

16. What can the grooming tactics tell you about the abuser and what they were trying to do to you?

17. Did different abusers use different tactics to control you?
Why do you think that is?

18. Grooming is extremely difficult to spot and most people never realise what the abuser is doing. Have you ever said the words 'I should have known'? Do you really believe that you should have known?

19. How did the abuser's grooming tactics change over time?

Impact of the abuse and trauma

This section contains questions about the impact of being abused, which may help you to explore the different areas of your life that have changed or been affected by being abused by someone.

Some responses to being abused or raped can include anger, fear, shame, sadness, shock, numbness, horror, feeling sick, feeling dirty, self-blame, guilt and confusion. However, if you were abused or raped by someone you believed you were in a relationship with or loved you, you might not have felt any of these emotions or responses.

For some of us, these emotions and responses only happen years later once we realise for the first time that we were abused or raped. Therefore, it is common for people subjected to sexual violence to experience no immediate trauma responses.

An example of this is when children are being abused by their parents, in which the child has been groomed to think that what is happening to them is normal, special or exciting. In lots of cases, these children will not display trauma responses for many years - or until they come to realise what is really happening to them. For some people, this can be in adolescence when they become more aware of sex and intimacy - or it can be much later. This often explains why people wait until adulthood to disclose or report childhood abuse, especially if they did not know they were being abused at the time of the offences.

The impact of being abused is often unique, wide-ranging and can fluctuate throughout the lifespan. For some women, it might mean that they become withdrawn, isolated, fearful and tired every day. For others, it might mean that they distract themselves with other activities, their career or their children.

Being sexually abused, assaulted or raped also challenges the worldview of most women and girls. The trauma of living through a rape, assault or a period of abuse can force a person to rethink everything they thought they knew.

Maybe the person who attacked them was their most trusted friend, their boss, their parent or their partner. Someone they looked up to. Someone they were inspired to be like. Someone they told all their secrets to. Someone they loved with all their heart. Suddenly, their feelings of safety, trust and judgement are shaken.

They consciously or subconsciously ask 'Who is safe? Who can I really trust? How did I not see that coming? Are all humans going to harm me? How do I protect myself from humans? Am I a bad judge of character? Why did they do this to me? Did I do something to deserve their harm? What if this happens to me again? Do I attract this type of person?'

Their view of sex might change too. Memories of being raped or abused might change the way they see sex. Sex may become scary, dirty, horrible, painful or may feel like a violation of their body again. Sex might feel like the ultimate act of trust. Sex might come with new rules, new boundaries and new feelings.

Women and girls might experience a change in their view of the world. A world that once held opportunity, excitement, adventure and a future might now start to look like an inherently dangerous and harmful place where no one is to be trusted and there is no future to look forward to. The world might have felt safe and filled with generally good people – but now feels like an unsafe place to live, filled with hidden sex offenders. The world might have been a positive place to live where the person felt they had self-efficacy and power over what happens to them – but now feels like a negative or uncertain place where the person feels powerless and at the mercy of random acts of violence.

The change in the world view of a woman or girl after sexual violence is often deep and long lasting – however, it is rational and reasonable. When we were evolving as a species, we encountered a new animal or a new threat and if it attacked us or harmed us in some way, we created a stereotype of that 'thing' and then we kept well away from it for the rest of our lives. We wouldn't have lasted this long as a species if we simply kept going back to the harm in the belief that it would be different this time.

When a woman or girl has been sexually abused, assaulted or raped, they process the features of the person who did it to them or the situation it occurred in and they often avoid those features whilst in trauma – and some avoid them for the rest of their lives.

Sexual trauma: physical harm and physical responses

It is important to discuss the physical ways the body responds during and after sexual assault, abuse or rape. This is very personal and variable. Part of this is based on acknowledgment.

Acknowledgement is whether the woman or girl knew they were being assaulted, raped or abused at the time of the offence. For example, a woman might think that she has no rights to say no to her husband so she must comply with his demands for extreme sex acts despite them hurting. Or a girl might have been sexually exploited for 5 months and not realise it until she is in her thirties.

In contrast, a woman might be raped whilst she cries and begs them to stop. Acknowledgement is at the heart of the response and the trauma – where someone has no idea they were being harmed, their physical responses to the crime will be delayed until they realise what happened, whether that is the next morning or five decades later. This is also why some people (including child abuse victims) can develop physical and psychological sexual trauma responses years after sexual violence.

In line with the work on physiological trauma responses in the body and brain, I am talking about the urgent release of noradrenaline which causes the increase in heart rate, blood pressure, the change in blood flow, the change in priority of blood supply to organs, muscles and extremities, the feeling of dizziness, the banging headache from the surge in blood pressure, the fainting or collapsing during or after the assault, the slowing of digestion whilst the body concentrates on keeping the person alive, the tingling of the skin, the sudden focus on their heart beat, the come down from the adrenaline leaving them shattered and unable to move, talk or focus on tasks.

These are just some of the common ways trauma can affect the body. These symptoms are not caused by an underlying medical problem. The person did not suddenly develop a serious medical problem in the weeks or days after being raped or assaulted. Instead, these are the ways that sexual trauma can impact the body – and the wide lack of understanding in professionals which leads to women and girls being tested for obscure medical issues, being prescribed medication for health issues they don't have and then, after years of searching for answers; being diagnosed with something that ignores the abuse and trauma.

Over my years in this field, I have become aware of some of the most common complaints from people who have experienced sexual trauma:

- Palpitations such as suddenly being aware of the heartbeat, the heart pounding, racing, fluttering or slowing

- Chest pains such as a stabbing sharp pain in the chest or a perception of 'heart pain'

- Muscle pains anywhere on the body

- Headaches and migraines ranging from tension headaches to days of severe migraine

- Fainting and collapsing which could include falls, losing consciousness momentarily, feeling faint but not actually fainting

- Digestive issues such as IBS

- Neck pain and shoulder pain

- Dizziness

- Tingling limbs such as fingers, arms, legs, feet, sometimes even one-sided in the face or lips

- Jaw aches and pains

- Pressure in the face or head

- Vertigo feelings

- Visual issues such as vision shaking, vision blurring, vision going grey

- Hearing issues such as losing hearing or everything going echoey before passing out

Whilst these symptoms sound terrifying, they can all be linked to or directly caused by the anxiety and trauma responses following sexual abuse, assault or rape. What makes this more complex and often even scarier for women and girls experiencing any of these symptoms is that they are often also linked with very serious physical health conditions such as stroke, heart attack, multiple sclerosis, diabetes, brain tumour and other rare conditions.

What this often leads to in the early stages is women and girls seeking urgent medical help (which all medical advice would advise for a lot of these symptoms, in order to rule out life threatening conditions) but getting nowhere. They get their clean bill of health from a confident medical professional who is sure that the symptoms are not life threatening and sent on their way.

In fact, this clean bill of health is not the reassurance the woman was seeking, and it often triggers health anxiety and the familiar googling of alternative diagnoses or the percentage of error in medical professionals. They get a clean bill of health whilst their symptoms spiral out of control and even develop into new symptoms. The medical professionals are confident that the symptoms are not life threatening (and they are correct) but they don't necessarily have any of the patient's trauma history, the knowledge to piece together the puzzle, the time or the resources to figure out that these symptoms are psychosomatic – and the person ends up on everything from beta blockers to proton pump inhibitors to treat the apparent 'symptoms'. The sexual trauma is never addressed, and the symptoms become embedded outlets for the anxiety, stress and trauma of their experiences.

All the symptoms above can be directly caused by high levels of stress, adrenaline and can therefore be linked to sexual trauma. Many of the symptoms are caused when the body is shoved into that 'fight or flight' mode day after day. High levels of cortisol and adrenaline increase blood pressure, heart rate, slow digestion, cause tingling in skin and limbs, change perception of pain and sensation, change visual processing and perception, change the priorities of the body and leave the person feeling like they are constantly on the 'edge' – some describe it as a constant impending feeling of doom or as if something terrible will happen at any given moment.

Muscles become tense and often take the brunt of trauma responses – commonly the neck muscles, shoulder muscles and the connecting muscles all across the head and face are tightened for days at a time, leading to searing headaches, pressure in the face, pressure in the temples, stiff neck, pulled shoulders and even jaw pain.

Fainting can appear serious – and due to the links with medical issues, it often leads to a trip in an ambulance (or ten). However, fainting after sexual trauma or at times of stress is a normal response for some people when they react to high levels of adrenaline in the body.

When women and girls who have experienced sexual trauma begin fainting, this is a sure symptom of stress that should be explored alongside any medical investigations. The body and brain has a complex and amazing relationship – meaning that there is debate as to whether the 'mind' shuts the body down to protect the person from further psychological trauma or whether the brain shuts down the body due to a sudden surge of adrenaline causing the momentary myopia.

When we put all of this information together, with the knowledge of experienced professionals who can recognise trauma responses after sexual violence – we can see that it is likely that hundreds, thousands or millions of women and girls will experience diverse trauma responses and may never find the professional who can help them to understand that their medical mysteries and boxes of unneeded medication are really due to completely normal, rational and common stress responses in human beings.

1. List all the different ways abuse has impacted your life

2. How did the abuse change you?

3. What has been the most profound impact on you?

4. What impact has abuse had on your relationships with others?

5. Write about how the abuse changed your confidence and self-esteem

6. How did the abuse impact you physically?

7. Write about the things you wish you could do, but don't do anymore since the abuse

8. How did abuse impact your sexuality and sex life?

9. How did the responses you got from your support network impact you?

10. How has the abuse impacted you on a day-to-day basis?

11. Did the abuse impact your education or career? In what ways?

12. Draw or doodle the impact the abuse has had on your mind

13. Draw or doodle the way the abuse impacted your social life

14. How has the abuse impacted your health?

15. Do you have any injuries, scars or reminders of the abuse that continue to impact you? How do you cope with that?

16. How has abuse impacted your trust of others?

17. How has the abuse changed your view of the world?

18. Discuss three things you think differently about having lived through abuse

19. Think about someone important to you. What do you wish they understood about the impact of the abuse?

20. Has abuse changed the way you think about particular people, places or events?

Trauma responses

This section contains questions and tasks about responses to trauma and abuse. It will ask you to consider what your own trauma responses are and what they mean.

When someone is being sexually assaulted, abused, raped or harmed in some way - everyone has different ways of reacting, coping or responding to that trauma in the moment it happens. Everyone also has a different way of responding immediately and in the days, weeks and months afterwards. There really isn't a right or wrong way of responding to being subjected to sexual violence.

Abuse and violence occur in lots of different contexts and is perpetrated by lots of different people. These factors influence how we respond and how we feel about the abuse or violence.

For example, we would probably respond differently if we were being abused by someone we loved and looked up to than how we would respond to being abused by someone we hated but we knew they were capable of hurting or killing us. In those two cases, we will still have some response to the sexual violence, but it might differ based on what would keep us the safest at the time.

Everyone responds to sexual trauma in different ways, which means some people worry about how they responded or reacted in the moment or in the hours and days after the abuse. It is common for people to question their responses and to wonder why they might have responded in a particular way. The most common question people ask is 'Why didn't I stop them?' or 'Why didn't I fight them off?'

Unfortunately, there is a lot of pressure on people subjected to sexual violence to be a 'model victim' who fights off the perpetrator and runs straight to a police station to report the crime. Most of us will never do this - but it doesn't stop us from feeling guilty or ashamed about our many different trauma responses.

Research has shown that we tend to measure our trauma responses against myths in society that we are supposed to fight back or shout for help. When we compare our experiences to the myths of the 'real rape' or the 'real victim', we often find ourselves not matching the rhetoric we are told to believe. For some women, this induces feelings of guilt, shame and blame.

How do people respond or react to sexual violence when it is happening to them?

Everyone is different.

However, practitioners and academics tend to talk about five adrenal responses that we have when we are threatened with danger. Our brains tend to perceive sexual violence as danger. However, some of us will not have a trauma response during rapes and abuse if we have been effectively groomed to believe that the abuser loves us or that we love the abuser. This means that for some of us, we could be raped or abused for long periods of time and not necessarily show any trauma responses until we are much older and have started to process what that person did to us.

For that reason, use the five F's with caution. Not everyone will experience them. Not everyone will have one set trauma response, either. In fact, most of us will be able to recall times when we have responded to different traumas in different ways. It is a myth that we have one default trauma response which is 'hard-wired' into our brains. We are much more complex than that.

The Five F's of Trauma

Fight - This trauma response is where we try to argue, fight, shout, push, kick, punch, swear, bite or any other response to being sexually abused or raped. It is a very rare form of trauma response in interpersonal violence. However, it is still seen by many as the 'first' trauma response - and so we are expected by society to have fought our attackers. Unfortunately, many of us have also been socialised to believe this myth too, which means we can often feel guilty or confused when we cannot explain or understand why we did not fight back.

Flight - This trauma response is where we try to avoid, escape or get away from the abuser or the abuse. We may try to do this in many different ways and does not mean we have to 'run' to have a flight response. Some people have flight responses they cannot act on, such as thoughts and feelings that tell you to 'get out' or 'leave', when you become aware you are in danger. Like 'fight', this response to trauma is rare. Most people do not escape a sexual assault or rape.

Freeze - This trauma response is the most common. 70% of us will 'freeze' during a rape or sexual assault (Moller et al., 2017; Eaton, 2019). A freeze response is one in which we feel as though we cannot move, cannot talk, cannot fight the person off or do anything to protect ourselves. People who freeze often do so to limit further harm from the perpetrator. However, this trauma responses often induces feelings of guilt because people feel as though they should have fought back.

Friend - This trauma response is where we try to talk or appease the abuser. Lots of us use this approach, especially those of us in long term abusive situations with parents, carers, partners or ex-partners. It is common for people who have a friend response to trauma to try to bargain with the abuser, to calm them down, to agree to one sex act but to ask not to be hurt, or to agree to something to protect someone else (including kids or family members).

Flop - This trauma response is argued to be a reaction to such high levels of cortisol (stress hormone) in the blood that our body shuts down non-essential muscles and body parts to keep us alive. This causes us to sort of 'flop', which some people describe as feeling like going limp, fainting, passing out or feeling like 'a rag doll'.

Whilst this list of trauma responses is helpful - remember that everyone is an individual and we were all abused or harmed in different situations. This means our responses will all have been diverse and purposeful at the time. It also means that you will not have one set trauma response that you always did or always do.

Your brain will respond differently based on what is likely to be the safest response at the time. For those of you with multiple perpetrators who harmed you, you might notice that you were more likely to try to talk one of them down, but there might have been one who was so violent and dangerous; that you were more likely to freeze until it was over. This is completely normal and very common.

All our responses to trauma mean something important. They are not just symptoms of distress; they are responses we developed to help us to survive or process the trauma whilst it was happening and after it happened. Trauma responses mean something individual to each person. Two people might have flashbacks but might have them for different reasons and might experience them differently.

The purpose of all our trauma responses is to warn us of danger and to make sure it does not happen to us again. For example, if after the sexual violence you found that you were left with a host of 'triggers', rather than seeing them as problematic or disordered; think of them as useful. Your brain is being triggered by those smells, sights, sounds or sensations to protect you from further harm. This was vital for us when we were prey in the wild. We needed to remember which events, animals, natural elements or experiences could kill or harm us. We remembered the feeling, sight, sound, smell of taste of impending danger so we could escape or protect ourselves.

Trauma triggers are doing the same thing. They are reminding us of factors that may protect us in future. For example, you may be left with triggers to men with a particular aftershave on, or cars of a particular colour and model, or the smell of cigarettes, or the taste of wine. These are important ways that our brain is trying to keep us safe.

1. How would you describe your own trauma responses?

2. Write down all the ways your body has responded to trauma

3. Make a list of things that trigger you back to a trauma response. As you go, make some notes about which ones seem worse/better/easier to control than others.

4. Which of your trauma triggers is the hardest to avoid in day-to-day life?

5. Over 75% of women freeze when they are raped or abused. Write about a time when you froze and why you think that happened

6. What does it feel like when you are triggered? Consider all five of your senses.

7. Which trauma responses confuses you the most? What do you think it means?

8. How would you describe your default trauma response when you are in danger of/actively being attacked?

9. Do you feel you understand your trauma responses and how they developed? Does understanding them help you to manage them at all?

10. Write about your trauma responses and how they worked to keep you safe during abuse or assaults

11. Have you previously thought that any of your trauma responses are abnormal or problematic? Why?

12. Have your trauma responses ever been mistaken for something else? What happened?

13. Which of your trauma responses kept you the safest and why?

14. Do you suppress any of your trauma responses? What caused you to do that?

15. Write about the last time you were triggered and why you think it happened

16. Have your trauma responses changed over time? How do you think they have changed?

Coping mechanisms for trauma and abuse

This section is about the way you cope with traumatic memories of abuse and violence. It follows on from the previous section about trauma responses.

The term 'coping mechanism' is used frequently to discuss the ways women cope with and attempt to manage the traumatic experience of being raped or abused. Dictionary.com defines a coping mechanism *as 'an adaptation to environmental stress that is based on conscious or unconscious choice and that enhances control over behaviour or gives psychological comfort'.*

Like trauma responses, all coping mechanisms have an important purpose. Coping mechanisms can be anything at all. Some of us might drink, take drugs, overeat, restrict food intake, self-harm, work too much, punish ourselves, overachieve, become perfectionists or even change something about ourselves to cope.

Some research (Morrow and Smith, 1995; Eaton and Paterson-Young, 2018) suggests that all our coping mechanisms really come down to two purposes:

1. To keep ourselves from being overwhelmed with feelings and memories we cannot cope with

2. To reduce our feelings of powerlessness, hopelessness and lack of control

This research is very important, because rather than perceiving our coping mechanisms to be mental illnesses or disorders, the research asks 'What is the purpose of this coping mechanism? What is it doing for this person?'

If a child who is trapped in abuse suddenly stops eating, we need to explore whether it is a coping mechanism or whether it is a way for the child to take back control of something in their life. Similarly, if an adult starts to drink to cope with the memories of the abuse, we must explore whether the drinking and disinhibition or relaxation is reducing the feeling of being overwhelmed.

Perceiving and processing our thoughts, feelings and behaviours as either trauma responses or coping mechanisms for the trauma is a key part of adopting a trauma-informed approach to understanding ourselves. Coping mechanisms mean something. They perform a protective role for us, either physically or psychologically. Coping mechanisms are not because we are crazy, disordered or abnormal - they always serve an important purpose.

Often, coping mechanisms develop during the abuse or sexual traumas and can continue for many months or years after you escape abuse.

For example, if you were abused for a long time by an unpredictable, aggressive person, one of your coping mechanisms may have been to become compliant, quiet and submissive. This may have worked many times to protect you from further violence or abuse, and then may become one of your coping mechanisms going forward. You may notice that you revert to this behaviour when people are being argumentative, confrontational or are becoming aggressive or loud around you.

Therefore, exploring where our coping mechanisms come from and when we first started using them can give us important insight into our thoughts, feelings and behaviours now.

1. List all your coping mechanisms for stress and trauma. When you have finished, consider which ones are healthy and which ones are harmful

2. Which of your coping mechanisms help you to feel more in control when you are traumatised? How does it do that?

3. Which of your coping mechanisms help you to escape? How does that work?

4. Write about how effective you think your current coping mechanisms are. What works and what doesn't?

5. How and when did your coping mechanisms develop?

6. All coping mechanisms have a purpose. List three of your coping mechanisms and then write about their purpose. What do they do for you?

7. Do you have any coping mechanisms that others perceive as harmful, but you find helpful or effective?

8. What do you think the long-term impacts are of using your coping mechanisms instead of processing the traumas?

9. Do you have any coping mechanisms that you don't like or wish you didn't have?

10. Which of your coping mechanisms got you through the toughest times? How did it help you?

11. What are your coping mechanisms protecting you from?

12. Do you have any coping mechanisms that appear positive or socially desirable to the outside world, but you know are harming you?

13. Which coping mechanism do you think you couldn't live without? Why do you think that is?

14. Have you ever tried to develop new coping mechanisms? How did that go?

15. Do you think some healthy coping mechanisms can become unhealthy coping mechanisms by overusing them?

16. What do you wish people knew about coping with trauma?

Victim blaming and self-blame

This section contains questions and tasks related your feelings of self-blame and your experiences of being blamed by other people.

Simply put, victim blaming is the transference of blame for an act of sexual violence away from the perpetrator of the violence and back towards the victim of the violence. In sexual violence, victim blaming includes the blaming of the victim's character, behaviour, appearance, decisions or situation for being subjected to sexual violence, rather than the attribution of blame towards the offender who committed the act.

Victim blaming is generally split into behavioural, characterological and situational blame; however, they often overlap.

Behavioural victim blaming blames the behaviour of the victim as the reason for the sexual violence perpetrated against them, whereas characterological blaming blames their character or personality for the sexual violence perpetrated against them. Situational blaming places the blame on the situation the adult or child was in, rather than blaming the perpetrator for choosing to commit violence.

Therefore, all victim blaming minimises or erases the actions and choices of the offender from their own offence. Messages of victim blaming have been found in the mass media, law, education, religion and cultural norms.

Why do people blame victims of sexual violence and abuse?

Theories of victim blaming are varied, and all try to suggest what motivates us to blame the victim. Generally, theories of victim blaming include the following:

Belief in a Just World

We victim blame because we have a strongly embedded bias that causes us to want to believe that the world is a just and fair place in which only bad things happen to bad people who deserve it. When a bad thing happens to someone, we attack their character or their behaviour to reframe them as a 'bad person' who made 'bad choices' so we can feel better about ourselves. We convince ourselves that we are good people who do not deserve bad things to happen to us, and we would not make the same 'bad choices'.

Attribution bias

We victim blame because we fail to attribute causation to negative events properly due to a cognitive bias. The attribution bias argues that we tend to blame internal issues for what happens to others and external issues for what happens to us. However, if this was true, this would mean we never self-blame.

Defensive attribution hypothesis

We victim blame when we perceive the victim to be very different from us (age, ethnicity, country, sexuality, culture). This theory argues that the more similar we are to the victim, the more empathy we have for them and the less we will blame them.

Rape myth acceptance

We victim blame because we believe myths and stereotypes about rape and sexual assaults. These myths mean we are more likely to believe women lie about rape or that there is a set of criteria that make up a 'real rape'. When the rape or abuse falls outside of these myths, we are more likely to blame victims of abuse and rape.

Sexism and misogyny

We victim blame because of a prejudice against women and girls. We blame the woman or girl for things that are inherently female or feminine. E.g. She was wearing a skirt, she was wearing too much make-up, she was too flirty, she led him on, she is promiscuous.

Perceived control and counterfactual thinking

We victim blame and self-blame because it makes us feel more in control of our safety and the world. We reason backwards to consider if our actions or decisions caused the rape or abuse. E.g. 'If I never went to my sisters, none of this would have happened!'

Does society encourage victim blaming?

The short answer to this question, is yes. Research (my own research and that of many others) has shown that there are many parts of society that encourage or maintain victim blaming in sexual violence and domestic violence.

Below is a list of institutions, factors and influencers that encourage or maintain victim blaming based on over 40 years of research:

- Criminal justice systems (from policing to lawmakers)
- Newspapers and online news sources
- Pornography
- Advertising
- Soaps and dramas
- Reality TV shows

- Education systems including schools and universities
- Social care services
- Health services including mental health services
- Sexism and misogyny
- Racism
- Homophobia
- Religions and faiths
- Cultural norms
- Families, friends and support networks

Victim blaming exists, is encouraged or maintained by every factor on this list. This makes victim blaming very common. Studies from the 1960s found that around 50% of the public believed that women brought rape upon themselves or lied about being raped to get revenge on men.

In 2005, Amnesty International found that a third of the public believed rape myths and victim blaming about people subjected to sexual violence. In 2011, McMahon and Farmer found that 50% of American university students believed that women 'ask' to be raped by the way they act or dress. In 2017 in the UK, the Fawcett Society found that 34% of women and 36% of men believed that women are partially or totally to blame for being raped.

In my own research between 2017-2019, I found that victim blaming was very common in men and women in the UK. Depending on the type of sexual violence, my studies showed that anywhere between 5%-68% of the British public blamed women for being subjected to sexual assaults, abuse, exploitation, rape and harassment.

When victim blaming is supported by so many different factors and institutions in society, these results are not surprising. However, this does mean that many people subjected to sexual violence will also be subjected to victim blaming.

What is self-blame?

'**Self-blame**' is defined as a cognitive process of attribution that tends to be defined based on two categories: behavioural self-blame and characterological self-blame.

'**Behavioural self-blame**' is the attribution of undeserved blame to self, based on behaviour or action. This type of self-blame leads to people considering how different behaviours or actions could have protected them or stopped the event from happening.

'**Characterological self-blame**' is the attribution of undeserved blame to self, based on internal character or personality. This type of self-blame leads to people believing that there is something internally or personally wrong with them that caused the event to happen.

Self-blame is also not unique to sexual violence, but studies have found that when people experience victim blaming or negative reactions when they disclose sexual violence, they are more likely to blame themselves. Further, existing research suggests that people subjected to sexual violence use the messages they receive from society and support networks to measure whether they think someone will blame them for sexual violence and to assess whether the rape, sexual assault or abuse was their fault.

With so many messages about victim blaming in society that we all receive from such a young age; it is no wonder that so many of us blame ourselves for sexual violence. Research shows that even children measure themselves against rape myths and victim blaming to decide whether they should report or disclose the abuse or rape. Recent research from 2019 showed that even young children believed rape myths and believed victim blaming messages.

However, there are lots of reasons why we might blame ourselves for sexual violence committed against us. I have provided some common examples for why people blame themselves for sexual violence below:

- To gain control again over the sexual violence and over our own feelings of safety. If we can blame ourselves, we can convince ourselves that we are in control and we can protect ourselves from the violence in the future.

- To punish ourselves for 'allowing it to happen' to us

- To "explain' why it keeps happening to us

- Abusers repeatedly told us that it was our fault, or we had brought it upon ourselves

- We felt love, lust or pleasure towards or with the abusers

- We feel we should have fought back more or done something differently to protect ourselves or protect others

- We were blamed by people who we believed and trusted (parents, carers, partners, authorities)

- We feel like we did something to deserve being raped or abused

People have many reasons for why they blame themselves. However, for others, they do not know why they blame themselves. Women I have interviewed told me that they logically knew they were not really to blame, but they still felt to blame. This is something I have written a lot about, because it suggests that self-blame does not sit at a logically, knowledge level - but at an emotional, deeper level.

1. How are women and girls blamed for being abused?

2. Why do you think victim blaming of women and girls is so common?

3. Write about a time when you were blamed for being abused or assaulted

4. How did societal victim blaming impact your understanding of what happened to you?

5. Lots of women who are blamed for being abused are told to change something about themselves to 'keep themselves safe'. Write about something you changed because you thought it would keep you safe from abuse

6. Have you ever questioned whether you are to blame for the abuse? How did that start?

7. Write a list of the ways the abuser would blame you for what they were doing to you

8. Draw a woman. Write around her all the ways she could be blamed for being raped.

9. List all the ways you have blamed yourself here

10. Are there any parts of the abuse you do not blame yourself for?

11. When did you first start to blame yourself and why do you think that happened?

12. Who encouraged you to 'take responsibility' for what happened?

13. List all the people and authorities who blamed you for being abused and how they made you feel

14. Would you blame another woman for being abused in the same way you blame yourself?

15. 'It is not a woman's responsibility to keep herself safe from rape. It is men's responsibility not to rape.' Discuss how you feel about this statement.

16. Write about a recent example of victim blaming you have seen or heard in the press

17. Do you think men and boys are blamed for being abused in the same way women and girls are?

18. How should we challenge victim blaming of women and girls in society?

19. What or who is encouraging women to blame themselves for being abused?

20. Write about the moment you realised that you were never to blame for the abuse

21. Who challenged your feelings of self-blame?

22. Who surprised you with their victim blaming beliefs?

23. Did you blame yourself for the abuse before anyone else blamed you, or did you only start blaming yourself after someone told you that it was your fault?

24. How do you counteract the self-blame thoughts?

Blame the abuser

This section provides space for you to think and write about the ways we should blame the abuser for their own choices and actions.

Not enough campaigns place 100% of the blame on the abusers and offenders. Instead, we often see campaigns which tell women and girls to live their lives differently, to keep themselves safer or to change something about their behaviour or character to avoid being abused.

I often wonder what the world would be like for all of us if we stopped making excuses for abusers and instead held them accountable. Further, I wonder what public campaigns, posters, adverts and educational resources would look like if they focused on blaming abusers for their choices, actions and thoughts.

The reality is that abusers are completely to blame for the crimes they commit against other people. No matter their own background, their own traumas or their own troubles – they should be held accountable.

One of the ways we can start to unpick the self-blame and victim blaming we have experienced is by putting the blame back where it belongs – with the abuser.

This section encourages you to blame the abuser for the things they made active, informed choices to do and say. Rather than seeing the abuser as making mistakes, losing control or not understanding the impact they are having – this section asks you to write about placing the blame on the abuser.

1. Write three choices that the abuser made that were not your fault

2. List all the things the abuser is to blame for

3. What do you wish the abuser would take responsibility for?

4. Use this page to tell the abuser what you think of them

5. Who should hold the abuser accountable for what they did?

6. Write about how the abuser would blame you for their own actions

7. Why don't we hold abusers 100% accountable?

8. What would change if abusers were blamed for their crimes?

9. How would you feel if the abuser admitted what they did?

Sex and intimacy

This section contains space to explore your thoughts and feelings about having sex and being intimate with another person after abuse.

When we have been subjected to sexual traumas and we disclose or seek help, lots of our conversations become about the rapes, abuse and assaults. Professionals talk to us about the sexual violence. Police talk to us about sexual violence. We think about the sexual violence. We can easily become engulfed by harmful and traumatic memories, conversations and images of sex. However, lots of us will go on to have healthy and happy sex lives. For this reason, it is important to have space to think and talk about having sex after sexual violence.

Secondly, it is completely normal and very common for our sex lives to be harmed by sexual violence and abuse we have been subjected to. Everyone is different in the way they cope with sex after sexual violence, but what is known is that most of us have never spoken to anyone about our sex lives after we were raped or abused. For this reason again, it is important to have information about having sex or being intimate after we have been abused by someone.

Can some people have good sex after they were raped or abused?

Absolutely. My research with 756 men and women subjected to sexual violence found that just over half of the sample said that they were able to have enjoyable, pleasurable sex with partners since they were raped and abused. However, this did mean that around half of those people were struggling to have good, enjoyable sex, too.

The key issue here seemed to be partners. People who were able to have good sex after rape and abuse had found partners who were respectful, who listened to them and who honoured their boundaries. This meant often asking them if they were okay, whether they consented and whether they were enjoying the sex. People who had partners who listened and cared about their experiences of sexual violence were having better sex too, especially where the person was able to tell their partner their triggers or boundaries.

Do other people get triggered or have flashbacks when they are having sex or being intimate?

Yes, this is very common. My research found that out of 756 people, 76% of them were having flashbacks or were being triggered during sex or sexual contact with partners. Over three quarters of people were experiencing these triggers and flashbacks.

This is normal, but most people reported them as being very distressing. Some triggers are easier than others to figure out. Some people knew what their triggers were during sex or sexual contact and avoided them at all costs (the smell of cigarettes, for example). However, others took years to learn their triggers or were still having flashbacks and triggers that they didn't understand or couldn't control.

How are people coping with having sex or being intimate?

Everyone was very different. Having sex meant different things to different people, and so their ways of coping differed too. Below are some of the most common responses to the research and how people explained they were coping with sex or being intimate:

'I don't have sex at all. I avoid it. I haven't been in a relationship since.'

'I get into relationships, but I don't have sexual relationships.'

'I get really drunk or high before I have sex.'

'I just grit my teeth and get on with it.'

'I cut myself after sex.'

'I only allow my partner to do certain things.'

'I told my partner what my triggers were and what I didn't want them to do and they listened to me. Now I am having the best sex in my life.'

'When I need to stop, my partner just stops and gives me a massive hug.'

'I don't know how to cope with it, I don't know what to do.'

As you can see from this list of real responses to the research, everyone was very different. However, there were some answers that were cause for concern. The answers about getting drunk, high, cutting themselves or gritting their teeth and getting on with it meant that none of those people were truly consenting to sex. We only consent to sex when we have full information, capacity and freedom to make a choice - and most importantly - when we really want to have sex. For lots of these people, they were having sex because they felt obliged to do so or felt they should. They were not enjoying it and were using lots of tactics to cope with sex they didn't really want to have. This is traumatic, too.

There were people who wrote that they were abstaining from sex or had made decisions not to get into any more personal relationships. This is completely normal and very common. There is no rule which states that we must be in relationships with people or have sex with people. Many people live long, happy lives whilst choosing not to have sex or intimate relationships. If sex is traumatic for us, or being in a relationship makes us feel worse, we do not have to put ourselves through either sex or relationships if we do not want them.

I think the abuse or rape changed my sexual preferences or sexuality - is this normal?

Lots of people in the research study wrote about the way the sexual violence had changed their sexualities, identities or sexual preferences. There is currently not a lot of research about this other than this one large study. However, it was a common answer in this large study. Men and women wrote about how they felt the abuse changed who they were attracted to, what types of sex they enjoy and how the abuse changed their own understanding of their identity.

From a trauma-informed perspective, it is rational and normal for the sexual abuse we have endured to change the way we feel about sex, our sexuality and the type of sex we enjoy or prefer. For example, there were people in the study who avoided sex with people who were the same sex as their abuser. There were also people in the study who wondered if the abuse influenced their attraction to a particular sex. Further, there were people in the data who were questioning their sexuality but were too scared to meet people of the same sex in case it triggered them. Whilst everyone was very different, sexuality and sexual preferences came up a lot in the data, with over 89% of the sample talking about this in their answers.

Should I tell my partner that I have been raped or abused?

This is absolutely your choice. If you are with a partner who has been respectful, open and non-judgmental about other personal matters and you feel you would like to talk to them about this, it is your choice to do so. Many people in the study found that when they had a loving and respectful partner, telling them that they had been raped or abused really helped their sex lives. However, some people in the study told partners and their partners did not support or respect them, which led to sex and relationships that were abusive and harmful.

However your partner reacts, it is not your fault and it is not your responsibility. If they do love you and respect you, they will listen, learn and respect your boundaries, wants and needs. If you do tell them about the sexual violence and they are not supportive, they do not believe you, they blame you or they ignore your boundaries - this is a red flag for an abuser and if you can, you need to do all you can to protect yourself and seek support to leave them.

Bear in mind that lots of partners don't really know what to say or how to support their partners when they disclose rape or abuse. If you have told a partner who loves you and respects you, but they do not know what to say or how to support you, it might be worth seeking support together. This is different from a partner who is uncaring or does not respect your boundaries.

1. What does sex mean to you?

2. How much enjoyment do you get from sex and intimacy?

3. How did the abuse impact your relationship with your own body?

4. Are there any parts of sex you don't enjoy anymore?

5. Have you ever been triggered during sex? What happened?

6. Do your sexual partners respect your boundaries?

7. Do you have any worries about your sex life?

8. What kind of sex or intimacy do you prefer?

9. What kind of sex or intimacy makes you feel unsafe?

10. Has abuse had any influence on who you are sexually attracted to?

11. Do you have any sexual preferences or fantasies that you feel might be related to the abuse?

12. Have you ever felt guilty or ashamed for feeling aroused or being brought to orgasm during the abuse?

13. Write about the kind of intimate touch you like and how you tend to communicate that to your partner

14. Do you tend to tell your sexual partners that you have been subjected to abuse? Have they been supportive?

15. Do you enjoy masturbation? Have you explored what you like since being abused?

16. What sexual activities can you no longer take part in or enjoy?

Pathologisation and medicalisation of women and girls

This section contains space to explore the pathologisation and medicalisation of women and girls who were abused.

A trauma-informed approach to understanding human distress is a way we can explore the trauma responses without medicalising the person. Instead of seeing the trauma responses as mental illnesses, disorders and abnormal behaviours, a trauma informed approach sees the trauma responses as normal, rational and purposeful. Therefore, the trauma-informed approach to understanding ourselves opposes the medical model of mental health. Instead, the trauma-informed approach draws on the social model of mental health, which argues that we should look at the context, environment and situations to explore trauma. The trauma-informed approach is anti-blaming and anti-stigma.

It is not 'what is wrong with you?'

It is 'what happened to you? what did someone do to you?'

Example: Medical model description of a person

Barbara has a history of child sexual abuse. She has been diagnosed with anxiety disorder, personality disorder and does not engage well with our services. We have tried to support her to open up about what happened, but she refuses to engage. She does not build relationships well, and often refuses to trust new staff members or support workers. She has attachment issues and is not ready for support.

Trauma-informed description of a person

Barbara was subjected to child sexual abuse. She is still very fearful and is struggling with trauma responses at the moment. She is not ready to talk to us about what happened yet, so instead we have supported her with other things she wanted to talk about. She is scared of new people and is not ready to trust any of us yet, this will take time and needs to be approached at her own pace, when she is ready.

You may be able to see clearly that the medical model diagnoses Barbara with psychiatric disorders, complains about her lack of engagement and self-help. Whereas the trauma-informed model does not seek to medicalise Barbara and instead sees her behaviours as normal and rational.

The trauma-informed approach would argue that trauma responses are not a mental health issue, a disorder, a psychiatric condition or problem. Instead, we choose to see trauma responses and coping mechanisms as healthy, normal, rational, expected and justified.

For example, it is healthy to be fearful and scared of abuse and memories of the abuse. It is normal to be traumatised by sexual violence. It is rational to fear it happening to you again and to change your behaviours to protect yourself. It is expected that you will have trauma responses after sexual and domestic violence. Your responses to trauma and your coping mechanisms are justified because what you have lived through was traumatic.

With this approach, trauma-informed theorists and practitioners do not perceive victims of abuse to be mentally ill, disordered or abnormal. They campaign against the medicalisation and pathologisation of adults and children who have been abused. Instead, they argue for trauma therapies, long term support and humanistic, holistic ways of supporting people without classifying them with mental illnesses they do not have.

This is still a very controversial way of working. The world is dominated by medical models of mental health in which professionals and the public are regularly told that mental health issues are due to brain chemistry, neuropsychology and imbalances. People are encouraged to go to medical professionals and seek medication for their traumas, with many people placed on waiting lists for support for months or years.

However, there are now many more psychologists, therapists, social workers and counsellors who are beginning to understand the trauma-informed approach and now campaign to stop the oppression and medicalisation of traumatised people.

1. Write about a time when you were told that you were mentally ill instead of being taught about natural trauma responses to abuse

2. Why are we so likely to diagnose women and girls with psychiatric conditions after they have been raped or abused?

3. If you told a doctor or nurse about the abuse, what was their response? Did they refer you to anyone for support?

4. Do you feel your trauma responses have been medicalised?

5. What if women and girls didn't have mental health issues at all, but were just processing years of abuse, trauma and harassment?

6. Which of your coping mechanisms or trauma responses has been pathologised or described as a disorder?

7. Why does society seek to silence and medicate angry women and girls?

8. Women and girls who had been abused and raped were often sectioned, medicated or tortured. Has much really changed?

9. Why are abused women and girls perceived to be so 'troubled'?

10. Isn't diagnosing abused women and girls as 'mentally ill' just another way to blame them?

11. What is society doing by telling women and girls that their responses to abuse are abnormal or disordered?

Sexism, stereotypes and misogyny

This section contains space to explore the way sexism, misogyny and the stereotypes of women and girls.

Sexism is defined as prejudice, stereotyping or discrimination based on gender (Oxford Dictionary, 2016). In addition, gender roles are defined as a set of socially constructed norms, generally derived from sexism, that dictate which behaviours and characteristics are considered acceptable or desirable based on gender. These messages and norms contribute to victim blaming and self-blame of women and girls by communicating a set of expected or accepted characteristics, behaviours and stereotypes of women – and of women and girls who are abused.

Hostile sexism is defined as overt misogynistic stereotypes and attitudes that position women as inferior to men, and used for sexual pleasure. Hostile sexism contributes to victim blaming by justifying the global exploitation of women as sexual objects and men's greater tolerance of sexual harassment of women.

Benevolent sexism is defined as sexism which appears positive or traditional, but patronises women using traditional gender role stereotypes to position women as weaker, helpless and cherished, vulnerable. This form of sexism has been found to elicit protection of traditional, gender role conforming women but hostility towards non-traditional, non-gender conforming women.

As gender roles are prescriptive, victim blaming increases when the woman is seen as not conforming to the perceived appropriate characteristics and behaviours of a woman. For example, Viki & Abrams (2002) found that when the characteristics of a woman were manipulated to describe her as contradicting gender role stereotypes of a traditional woman, she was blamed for the rape significantly more than when no information was given about her gender roles, marital or family status.

It has been recognised that some of prescribed traditional gender role characteristics of 'femininity' are contradictory. Women are expected to be submissive or passive in sex and yet simultaneously expected to control and preserve sexual activity. Women are socialised to be emotional, nurturing and submissive to men but also to fulfil their needs and to accept responsibility for limiting, causing and controlling men's sexual behaviours.

Women can therefore be blamed for being submissive or passive, controlling or preserving in sex depending on the situation. Females are expected to perform an identity that is 'sexy but not a slut' (Ringrose, 2013). Dichotomous gender roles and sexism provide a strong foundation for victim blaming beliefs about women 'asking for it' by what they were wearing or how they were acting. Gender roles are therefore instrumental in reinforcing a male-constructed, male-serving stereotype of a woman. When these strict social, cultural and behavioural boundaries are not conformed to, women can be positioned as to blame for sexual violence and harassment.

Recent research has shown that victim blaming, sexual violence tolerance and hostility towards the '#metoo' movement are all correlated with hostile sexism. Gender roles and sexism as theories of victim blaming of women are not only consistent and significant but should be seen as underpinning rape myth acceptance. Indeed, many of the rape myths are supported by both hostile and benevolent sexism, with gender role stereotypes and cultural pressures providing a fertile environment for rape myths to be developed, nurtured and communicated. Rape myths contain gender role stereotypes and sexism; and gender role stereotypes and sexism reinforce rape myth acceptance (Sleath, 2011).

When we talk about sexual intercourse, it is helpful to consider it within a radical feminist perspective. Sex has never been neutral for women and girls – sex has never been controlled by women and girls. Whether it's a father controlling when a woman has sex, the myth of 'losing her virginity', the media hypersexualising girls as early as possible with fashion and make-up, women being made responsible for contraception or being denied contraception and abortion, men being celebrated for being increasingly sexually active with many partners and women being punished for sexual activity and more than a couple of sexual partners, men being taught that women engage in 'token resistance' to sex, so if she says no, just keep badgering her... the list could go on and on forever.

These experiences of women and girls are caused by, encouraged by and maintained by sexism, misogyny and gender role stereotypes that impact women and girls, globally.

Sex is already wrapped up in so much power and control, so many expectations, rules and boundaries, so much shame, blame and honour. Women and girls are held up as sexual objects of desire and as chaste, pure virgins who should be sexually conservative; simultaneously. And these competing demands exist for women and girls having consensual sex with chosen partners.

Myths and messages about sex, abuse and rape therefore impact women and girls who have been abused.

Sexual abuse, assaults or rapes are rarely experienced as a form of sex. It is much more likely to be experienced as a form of violence, harm, suffering and fear. Despite this, many of the assumptions around sex are applied to rape, abuse and assaults. Women and girls are taught from an early age that they could have been 'asking for it' or they could have 'enjoyed it really'. They are told that they shouldn't have flirted, shouldn't have been polite to the man, shouldn't have accepted the drink, shouldn't have walked home with them, shouldn't have kissed them, shouldn't have swapped numbers, shouldn't have shared that taxi. In short, women and girls are made responsible for when 'sex goes wrong'. Women and girls are made responsible for the abuse, assaults and rapes committed against them.

1. How have you been impacted by sexism in your own life?

2. What is the stereotype of a woman who has been abused? Do you fit that stereotype?

3. What happens when a woman doesn't fit into the gender role stereotype?

4. Give five examples of misogyny you have experienced in your own life

5. How did misogyny and sexism support the abuser to commit their crimes?

6. What role is misogyny playing in the criminal justice process?

7. What happens if you are a victim of abuse but don't fit the stereotype of how a victim abuse 'should' look/act/speak/think?

8. List all the rape myths and stereotypes you can think of

9. Discuss all the ways misogyny is celebrated in society

10. Some people say that sexism is not an issue anymore. How do you feel about that?

11. What stereotypes were applied to you and how did it make you feel?

12. Why do we have such trouble acknowledging the violence against women and girls is rooted in global misogyny and sexism?

13. Why do we live in a society that encourages and profits from misogyny and sexism?

14. Why do so many people believe that women and girls lie about being raped and abused?

My advice to women and girls

This section contains scenarios and questions for you to consider what advice you would give to other women and girls who have been abused.

This approach can be useful for some women to explore whether they would advise others in the same (or different) way to the way they support themselves.

Often, our self-talk is different to the advice or support we would give to another woman or girl. There is good rationale for asking yourself what you would say to another woman in your position, to consider whether you are being too tough on yourself.

Read through the questions in this section and pick some to answer. What advice would you give to others?

Once you have answered these questions, consider whether you live by your own advice. Consider if you are kinder to other women and girls than you are to yourself.

1. What advice would you give to a woman who was still having nightmares 15 years after the abuse had ended?

2. What would you say to a girl who felt that she brought the rape upon herself by the way she was dressed?

3. What do you want to say to all women and girls about their feelings of self-blame?

4. Give your best tips to a woman who is struggling with panic attacks

5. What would you say to a woman who went to the police to report the abuse but felt the police blamed her?

6. What would you say to women who were currently stuck in abuse and were too scared to tell anyone what was happening?

7. What advice would you give to a woman who feels pressured to forgive the abusers?

8. What would you say to a girl who has not been offered any therapy, but has been told she has a mental health issue and has been offered medication after she was raped?

9. If a woman close to you told you that she had been sexually abused as a child and had only just remembered it, what would you say to her?

10. How would you support a woman who was harming herself to cope with the trauma of the abuse?

11. What would you say to a woman who told you that she hated her body since she was raped, and has decided she needs cosmetic surgery to 'correct' her body?

12. What advice would you give to a woman who was telling her daughters to cover their bodies unless they want to be raped on a night out?

13. What do you want to say to the government about the support needed for women and girls subjected to violence and abuse?

A letter to…

This section provides space to write letters to people who need to hear what you have to say.

This is a common approach in counselling and psychotherapy practice, and something that is often advised when women need to say something to someone, but don't necessarily want to do it in real life.

Some therapists encourage women and girls to write the letters they need to write as a cathartic process and then burn them, tear them up or hide them. Others might suggest writing letters to those people and then discussing them with the therapist or a close friend.

The letter writing exercises I have provided here may help you to find the words you have needed to talk about the abuse to specific people.

Remember that you never have to send these letters or do anything with them. They are simply a way of helping you to process trauma, abuse and feelings by addressing them directly to people in your life or who were involved in the abuse.

What you say to them in your letter is totally up to you.

1. Write a letter to your parents with everything you need to say to them about the abuse and the impact

2. Write a letter to someone who blamed you for being raped or abused

3. Write a letter to the abuser, telling them why you refuse to blame yourself any longer

4. Write a letter to a family member who failed to support you when you needed them most

5. Write a letter to yourself when you were being abused. Tell yourself what you needed to hear.

6. Write a letter to the professional who let you down

7. Write a letter to someone who supported you

8. Write a letter addressed to all women and girls about self-love and self-esteem after abuse

9. Write a letter to your partner or ex-partner about how they should have supported you better after abuse

10. Write a letter to yourself, ten years into the future. Tell her where you want to be and how you are going to do it

11. Write a letter to activists and volunteers who worked to set up the first ever rape centre

12. Write a letter to a woman who needs to know how to escape abuse safely

13. Write a letter to someone who needs to understand how you feel about the abuse

14. Write a letter to the family and friends of the abuser

15. Write a letter to the new partner of the abuser

16. Write a letter to the police officer you reported the abuse to

17. Write a letter to someone who helped you to think differently about the abuse

18. Write a letter to the world about global misogyny

Who I am today

A journal about processing abuse needs to include an entire section dedicated to who you are today.

Abuse changes us, sure. But abuse does not define us. We are not the abuse. We are not merely abuse victims. We still have thoughts, dreams, opinions, hobbies, skills, education, experiences and beliefs. We still have so much to give to the world, to our loved ones and to ourselves.

This section is all about you.

Write about yourself and enjoy it.

1. Write five things you are good at

2. Describe what kind of friend you are

3. Discuss something kind you did for someone else

4. What do you enjoy doing?

5. How do you relax?

6. Who are the most important people in your life?

7. What goals do you have for the future?

8. Write about your biggest achievement to date

9. Write about your favourite place in the world and why it is your favourite

10. Write about your key strengths

11. List five social causes or issues that you care about

12. What is your favourite song and why?

13. List all the places you want to visit

14. What is your favourite book and why?

15. What is something you cannot live without?

16. What is your favourite quote about life?

Draw yourself

This section contains ample space to get your doodles flowing. Whether you will spend time drawing intricate cartoons or artwork – or whether you will doodle, scribble and stick-figure your way through these tasks – have fun with it.

Doodling and drawing can help you to think differently about issues that might be difficult to write about.

They say a picture is worth a thousand words, you know.

1. Draw yourself as a world leader, announcing your new policies

2. Draw yourself overcoming trauma

3. Draw yourself rebuilding yourself and your life after you escaped the abuser

4. Draw yourself rising above societal expectations of you

5. Draw yourself smashing the patriarchy

6. Draw yourself with the people you love most

7. Draw yourself talking to your younger self

8. Draw yourself much bigger and much more powerful than the abuser

9. Draw yourself in five years' time

10. Draw your journey through trauma and reflection

11. Draw yourself surrounded by other women who have lived through abuse

12. Draw yourself protesting violence against women and girls

13. Draw global misogyny

14. Draw a feminist conference full of women from all walks of life

15. Draw what the world would look like if women were believed and supported after rape and abuse

16. Draw yourself then and now

Eek! You have finished your Woman in Progress journal!

How do you feel?

Wherever you are in your journey, please know that you are not alone. You are not to blame for abuse you were subjected to. You are much stronger than you will ever realise.

Love,

Jessica

Where to seek further support

Sexual Abuse Referral Centres – Find a SARC online by googling your area and the acronym 'SARC'

SARCs are specialist medical and forensic services for anyone who has been raped or sexually assaulted. They aim to be one-stop service, providing the following under one roof: medical care and forensic examination following assault/rape and, in some locations, sexual health services. Medical Services are free of charge and provided to women, men, young people and children.

Rape Crisis

Helpline: 0808 802 9999 (12-2:30 and 7-9:30)

rapecrisis.org.uk

National organisation offering support and counselling for those affected by rape and sexual abuse. See website for local groups or contact directory enquiries.

Victim Support

Supportline: 0333 300 6389

Our services are confidential, free and available to anyone who's been raped or sexually assaulted, now or in the past. We can help, regardless of whether you have told the police or anyone else about the attack. Our volunteers can visit you at home (if you want us to, and if doing so will not put you at further risk) or somewhere else if you prefer. If you don't want to see anyone face-to-face, you can also talk to us on the phone, either at one of our local offices or at the national Victim Supportline.

RASAC (Rape and Sexual Abuse Support Centre)

National Helpline: 0808 802 9999 (12-2.30 & 7-9.30)

rasasc.org.uk

National helpline for survivors of rape and childhood sexual abuse, their families and friends. Provides emotional and practical support.

Women Against Rape

womenagainstrape.net

This is the joint website of Women Against Rape and Black Women's Rape Action Project. Both organisations are based on self-help and provide support, legal information and advocacy. We campaign for justice and protection for all women and girls, including asylum seekers, who have suffered sexual, domestic and/or racist violence.

The Survivors Trust

Helpline: 0808 801 0818

thesurvivorstrust.org

Rape and sexual abuse can happen to anyone regardless of their age, gender, race, religion, culture or social status. Living with the consequences of rape and sexual abuse can be devastating. We believe that all survivors are entitled to receive the best possible response to their needs whether or not they choose to report.

Women's Aid

National Domestic Violence Helpline (24hrs): 0808 2000 247

womensaid.org.uk

Women's Aid is the national domestic violence charity that helps up to 250,000 women and children every year. We work to end violence against women and children, and support over 500 domestic and sexual violence services across the country.